AT THE GATE

Mike

AT THE GATE

Ann Gray

very best wishes
Ann x

(loved The aquarium!)

HEADLAND

First published in 2008
by
HEADLAND PUBLICATIONS
38 York Avenue, West Kirby,
Wirral, Merseyside. CH48 3JF

A full CIP record for this book is available
from the British Library

ISBN 978 1 902096 49 0

Printed in Great Britain by
Oriel Studios, Orrell Mount
Hawthorne Road
Merseyside L20 6NS

HEADLAND acknowledges the financial
assistance of Arts Council England

CONTENTS

CONTENTS *continued*

Acknowledgements

Some of these poems have previously appeared in *The SHOp, The Rialto, Tears in the Fence, Poetry Pool 4, In The Red* and *Acumen*.

"Your Body" was highly commended in the *Forward Anthology 2008*.

Huge thanks to my children, their partners and wives, for their comfort and encouragement, my brilliant sisters, to Beth and to Nick, Edmund Cusick, who patiently read each poem as it was written, to Tony Lopez, to members of the Liskeard Poetry Group for their loyal support, to Ruth, and to Lynne, for the gift of laughter. Grateful thanks to Gladys Mary Coles for her continuous support and to Michael Scott's wife, for allowing me to use his painting, 'The Lovers'.

The artist **Michael Scott,** was born in 1946 and grew up in two of Britain's once busy fishing ports: Peterhead and Hull. He lived and worked with his wife and family in Glasgow from 1969 where he combined university teaching with painting. His work is held in collections around the world. *'The Lovers'* was completed in the year before his sad death in 2006 and shows his unending belief in humanity, hope and love. His admiration for the power of poetry underlay his agreement to use the reproduction of the painting for this anthology.

For Alan

We lift our glasses in *The Rubicon.*
Garnet Wine. I've lived my life inside out,
upside down and backwards. You tell me
this is simple. This is how it is. I'm going
to have a shot at monogamy. I like
the way it sounds, now. First and last.

From *The Man I was Promised*

Could it have been Northampton Street?

It's 3am and I think about the silk
of your skin. I think about the size
of your hands, the way you mutter
in the night and grab me.
I don't count sheep, but wrestle
with road names, Magdalene Bridge,
Magdalene Street, Castle Hill,
the traffic lights where the 101 bus
turned right to Chesterton,
or was that the 105?
I'm seventeen, at this place,
whatever it's called,
it's September, before the start of term,
there is absolutely no traffic,
just us, you lean on your bike.
You ask me to come to a party.
I hug myself all the way home.
You are 2 years older,
you take your guitar to parties,
everyone begs you to play,
La Bamba, Big Bamboo,
everyone sings, you are the party.
I hug myself all the way home.
At the party, you play, we dance.
We sing along with the Beatles,
and you swoop down to kiss me.
Your kiss is the kiss of a feather.
I carried my half of that kiss
for 34 years, and came to find you.
I found you had carried yours.
How could you leave me now?

When we met again, everyone we knew
wanted a part of our story. My little sister
remembered she'd sat on your knee,
that you'd held her in the small of her back
on her bike, so she could ride uphill faster.
My little brother said you told him a Good Joke
about Australia and he took it to school.
My other sister said, he was nice, I bet he is now
and I bet he still loves you. Everyone remembered
your bike, how you rode out to see me, then
we rode in, rode back, you rode home; twenty miles.
Looking back, that would explain your glorious legs,
why I couldn't leave them alone and why
you were late for athletics, how you always said
I cost you a Blue. My nephew said we'd
escaped from *When Harry met Sally*, would talk
about finding each other, toothless and ninety.
My German cousins were there the day you came
and I had to explain why I couldn't stop grinning.
I should have known you'd be late, even an hour
and a half didn't stop me wanting to see you
stooped on the step, exactly as always, but older.
I took you to Beckett and we sat for two hours
without touching, except the hairs on our arms,
until I asked to kiss you. You were shy,
out of practise, but you wished that I would.
Later we ate, somewhere outside, later still,
by the river at Chelsea, you asked me to breakfast.
I remember you showed me our black and white photo.
I remember the shock, the pain in my chest
and the tears that surprised me. We both cried.
You said, tell me how you want to be loved.
You asked me to show you. I remember
the smell of your bed, the look on your face,
how you said, how long will it last?
how I said, I can't tell you that now.

Fat with Fruit

Being loved changed me,
gave me an awareness of orchards,
wild orchids, cowslips in the grass,
birdsong, hives of bees, honey, my love,
the quiet light of evenings,
sitting before sleep.
I was fat with it, with words for fruit –
Winter Nelis, Swan's Egg, Longkeeper.
I planted them on paper, measured
distances they'd need, shelter, sun.
Red Roller, Tommy Knight,
Burcombe cherries. Plums.
Cornish Gillyflower, Polly Whitehair.
Pears, if only for their blossom,
their blossom alone.
I planted an orchard
in my late summer,
early autumn, fat with fruit.

Crackington Haven

It's late and I'm spilled out
with the last gold of the sun

in streamers on the sea.
The sand is striped in shadow.

We leap the scarcely waves
until we're wet beyond our shoulders

and have to swim. Time always
stretches us in all directions;

before, now, what we will be.
Everything can be lost here

in the slippage of the light,
the darkening land.

The sea steals in to flood the river.
I am weightless, could swim

for nights and nights
if you were close, could wake me,

turn my terrors inside out
and make them seamless.

Until Now

Everywhere I've been
I've imagined being somewhere else,
waiting for that moment a hillside bursts
through peat as cinnamon to water
and all the sound is silence;
white bones picked clean on a coral shore.
This is North. North West.
The Hebrides fade in, fade out.
Snow lingers on the mountains.
The day is longer, more distinct, more silver.
The moon's eleventh hour is breathless.
It no longer matters how or why,
before this I was single.

Your Body

I identified your face
and when he said is this, and gave your full name,
it wasn't enough to say, yes, he said I had to say,
this is, and give your full name.
It seemed to be all about names, but I only saw your face.
I wanted to rip back the sheet and say, yes this is his chest,
his belly, these are his balls and this the curve of his buttock.
I could have identified your feet, the moons on your nails,
the perfect squash ball of a bruise on your back,
the soft curl of your penis when it sleeps against your thigh.
I wanted to lay my head against your chest, to take your hands,
hold them to my face, but I was afraid your broken arm was hurting.
My fingers fumbled at your shirt, the makeshift sling had trapped it.
Your shirt, your crisp white shirt. The shirt I'd ironed on Friday.
The shirt that grazed my face when you leaned across our bed
to say goodbye. I watched the place where your neck
joins the power of your chest and thought about my head there.
He offered me your clothes. I refused to take your clothes.
Days later I wanted all your clothes. I didn't know what I wanted,
standing there beside you, asking if I could touch you,
my hands on your cheek. He offered me a lock of your hair.
I took the scissors. I had my fingers in your hair.
I could taste the black silken hair of your sex.
I wanted to wail all the Songs of Solomon,
I wanted to throw myself the length of you and wail.
I wanted to lay my face against your cheek.
I wanted to take the blood from your temple with my tongue,
I wanted to stay beside you till you woke.
I wanted to gather you up in some impossible way
to take you from this white and sterile place to somewhere
where we could lie and talk of love.

I wanted to tear off my clothes, hold myself against you.
He said, *take as long as you want,* but he watched me
through a window and everything I wanted seemed
undignified and hopeless, so I told him we could go,
we could leave, and I left you
lying on the narrow bed, your arm tied in its sling,
purple deepening the sockets of your eyes.

My Dearest Dust

Lady Catherine Dyer 1641

What is a body - but meat and bone?
Yet for six days I'd wait to be alone
with you at dusk, when all the day was done,
whatever rain had rained and sun had gone.
My love, I gave away your eyes, but you
could see, I gave away your heart, but knew
it still belonged to me. Your hair still grew.
The stubble on your chin made me argue
part of you still lived - and so I spoke
to you of love, my loss, and through the smoke
of tears, I lifted back the robe to stroke
your hands, your fingers set, in case you woke,
stretching to find a chord, to dive headlong
into a blast of noise, for one last song.

Any day now

How do I tell the dogs
when every time they hear a guitar
they leap from their beds
to run rapturously through the house,
when every Thursday they guard the door,
ears lifted for that particular sound of car,
footsteps on the gravel, the way you'll laugh,
bending double to pull their ears, rough their fur,
before you straighten up to kiss me,
sling your bags across the table and struggle in.
How do I tell the dogs
when they believe you're coming,
if not today, then any day now.

mercifully ordain that we may become aged together
Tobit 8.7

I was in the Canadian Muffin Company in Armada Way,
waiting for an extra large latte, cinnamon and chocolate
and a white chocolate chip muffin, to take away,
when I saw them. He was helping her get into her coat.
He held it out for her as if the sleeves were winged
while she gracefully turned her back to shrug it on.
At this point he did a little jink, more of an imperceptible
hoick, on the balls of his feet, so the coat lifted
neatly over her shoulders and tucked under her neck,
then he freed her hair from the collar. He must have
done this for years, this exact same thing for years.
I watched him pick up the shopping, she picked up
her bag, and I collected my latte and my white
chocolate chip muffin and walked out into the rain.

For Edmund

All those things we did that never happened
is why I trust you now,
watch you unlace my shoes,
tell me Annwn is one day's ride
from here, and we will find him,
his legs beneath the table, a jug of wine
beside him. He will have the memory
of everything of me, and he will tell stories
of planting orchards, or travelling to find me.
He will tell them how it felt to hold me
in the night, and he will take up his guitar
to sing about it. You say he doesn't weep
as I do, because, at the moment that he left,
he knew I loved him and he was safe in that.

Pyjamas

I found the racks of nightwear, sat and wept.
I couldn't stand, my legs were sand and hurt,
I found I'd been abandoned while I slept.

The air was carolled, every shop was packed.
My chest was tight, my mouth was furred with dirt.
I found the racks of nightwear, sat and wept.

We'd chosen gifts, we had them wrapped and stacked.
With just another week to live apart,
I'd found I'd been abandoned while I slept.

I bought a woollen vest. Before you left
you'd always held me naked to your heart.
I found the racks of nightwear, sat and wept.

I tried to think pyjamas, thought bereft.
There were pyjamas there. I never thought
I'd find I'd been abandoned while I slept.

I didn't want pyjamas, blue or checked,
but just to sleep forever with your shirt.
I found the racks of nightwear, sat and wept
to think I'd been abandoned while I slept.

Harvest

I open her letter. I remember her call,
a shopping list that started, two eyes,
one whole heart and used the verb,
to harvest. She gave me the HIV spiel,
how they have to test for it, how
if you had it then they would have to tell me
and did I think you had it, and I said, No.
She said, so he was a good boy then?
I said, pardon me?
She said, so he was a good boy then?
That's what I thought you said, I said.
I think of you, a good boy.
I slide my hands over your skin.
I look out at the magnolia stellata, silver,
I look out at the red and pink camellias,
I look out at the peach tree, flowering against the wall.
Her letter thanks me, on behalf of a family,
on behalf of a man of 27, who can see,
and I thank you, thinking, today would be
a good day to see, for the first time.

On top of the world

It could have been perfect.
We wove our footprints in the sand for you to see
and, screwing our eyes to the blast of sun-dazzle
we wondered if, where you are, the sun is always
splayed out across the sea. We kicked at bladder-wrack
played leaping games with sticks, stones, dodged waves,
until I stopped, turned, took a moment to contemplate
the absolute blueness of the sky, stood still long enough
for a breaker to smack me in the small of my back
and fill my socks. I drove home on a map of the world,
soaked, two salty dogs, shattered, in the boot.

Lantic Bay

six hundred and forty four steps down
to swim across the bay
the blue bowl of the sky
fringed with corn

six hundred and forty four steps down
to sit here
to eat plums
from a juice soaked bag

six hundred and forty four steps down
to see you hurl yourself
at the waves
to hear you sing

how sweet it is to be loved by you
to hear you shout
it's cold cold cold
come in come in

I sift the whitest stones through my fingers
the only song is in the pounding
of the water   there are six hundred
and forty four steps back up

with every breath   I count them

The bed's too big, the frying pan's too wide

The platinum rabbit makes a noise and smells of plastic.
One photo shows your inner upper-arm. I taste it.
I let my fingers find you. It begins, this is the best one,
seventeen, in Bridget's flat, with half our clothes on.
I press my forearm to my eyes to make the darkness
more intense, but then I've lost it. Wait, you undress,
I'm eighteen, in your rooms, on a ropey sofa,
someone's banging on the door, shouts and laughter.
I lift myself to fifty-four, to fifty-six, I hold your face,
it's always been all about me, every time, every place,
your name is now unstoppable, I shout, I scream,
I want it back, I want you now, I want this thing
called - and then it's over, my whole life is over
and someone out there fries bacon for a lover.

Fox

The dogs are frantic, smell fox
long before I find my first hen,
stiff in the nettles.

Surely the cockerel with his fantastic tail
put up a fight, the drake, for his three
long-necked beautiful duck wives.

I consider the carnage,
one carcass, picked clean,
caught on the wire,

a string of neck bones
and one webbed foot.
You named these birds.

It's by these names I call them
as I lift their desperate legs
pooled in the fight of feathers.

The cockerel was a gift, white,
shuffled in amongst the Black-Rock hens.
The ducks were barter for all the beer

drunk, that long-gone summer.
Four Indian Runners
who could not run fast enough.

I walk the fence, find the tunnels,
the shallow dips of dry earth.
I tell myself I can't cry for hens.

I tell myself I can start again,
coop them up, keep them safe,
never see their joy, scratching

their way through the orchard,
strutting amongst the cherry trees,
chin high in campion and clover.

In Dreams

Some nights I dream out of a need this pure
it cracks me open, it leaves me breathless.
I have seen you. I wake fragile, unsure,
confident of nothing, my life a mess.

It cracks me open, it leaves me breathless.
I wake sweating, I grope for your hands.
Confident of nothing, my life a mess,
I'm at the window, I can barely stand.

I wake sweating, I grope for your hands.
It's four in the morning. The birds still sing.
I'm at the window, I can barely stand.
O, pretend you live. O, pretend you'll ring.

It's four in the morning. The birds still sing.
I pour myself water and watch the day.
O, pretend you live. O, pretend you'll ring.
I dream of you, watch my life slip away.

I pour myself water and watch the day.
The day unfolds itself against the sky.
I dream of you, watch my life slip away.
I close my eyes. I want the day to lie.

The day unfolds itself against the sky.
I have seen you. I wake fragile, unsure.
I close my eyes, I want the day to lie.
Some nights I dream out of a need this pure.

Last night we danced.

We dance often.
Our foxtrot is immaculate and delicious.
We whirl and twirl
two inches above the parquet floor
of the Dorothy Ballroom.
Do you remember the Dorothy Ballroom
on the corner of Sidney Street?
We never went there.
Sainsbury's was underneath.
I went there with my mother and sister.
We caught the 106 bus.
Everything had its own queue.
We bought 6 cracked eggs in cardboard.
I said, half a pound of greenback bacon
to a man with a white apron and hat.
We never tire of this whirling and twirling.
Sometimes I stand on your feet.
You are tall and we move faster.
You never answer your phone.
Once or twice, you have returned
to hold me. You move above me
in a pool of white heat, silent.
I say, It's you, it's you, it's you.
Once you went to Spain.
I could see you in Granada,
you walked to Lorca's house, eating oranges.
Once you had an incurable disease
and thought it better to be absent.
When you told me, I said I wanted
to be with you, even if you were dying,
especially if you were dying.
Once you walked up behind me,
put your hands on my shoulders.
I touched your fingers, the nails
filed sideways for flamenco.
That night I didn't let myself believe it

and I didn't turn round.
I was sick of this whirling and twirling.
You always die. One night
I found the band you played in.
I spelt out my name.
They said you'd spoken of me,
you'd planned to get in touch.
That night I woke myself up.
The bedroom was an upturned
boat, solid as lettuce,
and when I spoke to you
you didn't answer.

A hot country

Once we went to a hot country,
we danced in the market square,
blue flags and scarlet bunting.
There was a makeshift band.
We bought brown bread, fruit, wine.
I said, for some part of every year,
I will live here. This made you happy.
We kissed, sitting on the pavement.
You held your soft mouth open
until it drove me to distraction.
We took the flapping sides
of a green parasol to make a tent.
It opened to the shingle of a beach.
You took the cork from the red wine
with your teeth. You drew yourself up
to your full height, flexed your shoulders.
Two shots rang out. The dogs barked,
and I woke to hear the wind
rattling at the summer ash keys,
punishing the garden umbrellas.

La Alhambra
entre el cielo y la tierra

We stood in the forest of columns.
This is what I remember,
not the Sierra Navada,
the Generalife gardens, not the water,
not the rooms where the sun fell as stars,
not us, together, a few precious days,
but a pack of black demons
screaming and scything their way
through the patio de los Leones,
their sickle wings cutting the air,
reclaiming the palace for May;
Devil's birds, vencejo,
ababil, apus apus, black swifts
condemned to continuous flight.
I want to remember the fountains,
long ponds of fish, but I always see swifts.

Code

All I want to do is see you again.
I'm wrestling with the secret of the code,
the time, the date, the place, the dark, the rain,
the exact spot your car flew off the road,
but the strange geometry might mean that I
calculate the square root of the weather
divide it by the lorry, multiply
your speed by your distance from the river.
Even if these variables were exact
I could still miss-time it by a second,
the year can never be the same, that fact
is insurmountable, so I'm lost, and
what if I saw you in the distance when
you couldn't see me, what would I do then?

Better together

I've walked these woods in every weather,
through rain drenched grass and soaking clover,
in hail and snow and growling thunder,
the south west wind my only lover,

seen all the different tides of water,
mud-flats, full in, swollen, silver,
the ranks of trees a lasting coda.
I've looked for signs I could decipher

one green egg, a buzzard feather.
May happened faster than I remember,
the beech trees swam in blue, and further
in, the violets called me to either

cry, or pray, were I a believer.
I haven't lost my sense of wonder
through cloying gorse, thick as sugar,
the early broom, the vetchling, heather,

the yellow iris by the river.
Three thousand miles and I'm no wiser.
The hours of light are getting longer,
swallows streak in to speak of summer.

I call the dogs, they race each other
to cover me in mud and slobber,
and, driving home, we dream of hunger,
as Jack Johnson sings, *Better Together.*

One night you'll come back and I'll wake
to see you moving noiselessly in your socks,
you'll look bewildered, nothing's quite the same.
You'll be hunting through the drawers,
wondering where your clothes are.
I won't move or speak, I'll try not to breathe.
I'll want to say, look in the wardrobe,
I saved your Levi boots and leather jacket.
I'll watch you lift photos in their frames,
take them to the window. Some faces
you won't know. You'll guess at Beth.
I'll watch you sink to your knees,
cover your head with your hands.
I'll hear you whisper, Nick. Nick got married.
I'll watch you disappear to the bathroom,
hear you brush your teeth, hear you pee,
see you reappear with a glass of whisky.
You'll sit on the edge of the bed for ages,
until you turn to lift my hair, touch my neck,
then hold your mouth there.
Then you'll say, so what happened?
and I'll say, how long have you got?

Churchbridge

If Arcadia is where you are, you
must be here, in this jewel of a field.
Here, where the forest opens itself. Few
have found it, seen the Ladies' Smock, a world
of lilac, the buttercups waist high, more
yellow than you can imagine yellow.
Dog roses bloom in the elderflower,
Marsh Iris unfurl, as I walk the slow
afternoon hours, as the dogs swim upriver,
their pale legs balletic underwater.
I lift my eyes to the oval sky, offer
myself up to its intense liquid blue, to
ask you again, if you could come back soon,
to share this, this extraordinary June.

Yunnan Gold

Somewhere in that blur of a year,
I discovered there'd been a live
transaction on your card cancelled,
a thin plastic bird, catapulted down
in mid-flight, its mission aborted.
A year later, in this bold moment,
I email and find your order,
your message: *more Morning Tea
- for drinking hot or cold...*
a Christmas present I never had.
Hunched over the keyboard,
I see you climb back into bed,
burrowing under the duvet,
kissing each knot of my spine
until I turn to you, drowning.
I hear you say, *I've brought you tea,
do you want to drink it hot or cold?*
Hand-made amber tea from the South China
Vietnam border, eight hundred years old,
a taste of pepper.   I read: *allowed
to take one tea to a desert island,
Yunnan Gold would be our clear choice.*

Yunnan Gold. Cold.

CCTV

Each frame freezes long enough to seem robotic.
We watch a woman stacking shelves on her knees.
The door opens and you come in. *There he is,*

our voices lift with joy, as if you were returning.

We watch you chose a fizzy drink, sandwiches,
stooping at the chiller. I guess BLT, the policeman says,
three cheese savouries. That figures, if there were

no BLT that day. You rest one elbow on the counter.

You sign your name. I think you smile, but the jerky
black and white is grainy. I want to weep.
My throat aches, but I'm shelled out, dry with despair.

It all seems such a long time ago. You don't know Jago.

You don't know Janie's pregnant. You weren't in Prague,
Milan, the Cinque Terra. I think this in a small room
with two of my sons and two policeman in full uniform.

I had asked to see this on my own, to watch you more intently.

We're here to understand the how, the why, the when.
Today's the day I can ask questions. The coroner nods
in my direction. I shake my head. I've been asking questions

all this year. Where are you now? Can you see me?

All those parties

It's your birthday. We're doing lunch.
I've brought two chocolate cakes
and far too much champagne.
Everyone is late, subdued and careful.
Last year was worse. We ate at Arthur's,
on the Green, your empty chair between us,
cut your cake at home, but didn't sing.
I crept into your cold bed and lay awake
till morning. I folded all your socks in pairs,
took some books and drove away
while your whole road was sleeping.
Today, you're sixty. We lift our glasses.
I make the Spanish Toast and want to leave.
Your big sister holds me, standing by my car.
We have no words for this. Miles later,
I'll pull over and throw up in a hedge,
think of all those parties, all those years ago,
when someone always cried, someone was sick.

Crackington Haven 2005

It isn't your last breath, beside the road,
your ashes by the trees, where you are
most alive for me, but at here at Crackington.
I'm standing in the sea, in the December sun
with five red roses to mark each year
and one white rose for this first year apart.
I throw my flowers to the swell and tell you
this is how it is. I throw the white rose last.
The tide carries them out, then in again,
curling across the sand, caught in the froth,
the spume, the uneven drag and swirl,
an art-house film that would have music
to tell us how to feel, violins and piano.
I offer you everything I've written this year
as I read it to the wind, the nifty breeze
that's whisking round the headland.
I cast my love for you upon the water.
The sea pulls further and further out
beyond the rocks, until the scarlet heads are lost,
and I turn to trudge the sand-filled bay,
head down, squinting through the salt.

"If you want to come after me for any reason,
I have left money in the bread-box..."
W.S.Merwin

I walk the long road to Aussonne,
the long road through the cornfields.
I sing, *oats and beans and barley grow.*
The baby holds pink and white convolvulus.
We squat to watch striped bees
feeding on blue mallow.
We watch polka-dot butterflies.
The dragonflies are a greyish silver.
We collect pinecones, colts-foot,
blue fringed teasels.
We sit with our feet in a ditch,
eating blackberries.
These are his first blackberries.
He wrinkles his nose,
then he shouts, more, more.
They are cutting the corn.
The men nod their heads, Madame.
The baby waves from his pushchair.
Buzzards follow the tractors.
The baby makes a thin melodic noise
and kicks his legs.
I sing, *one man went to mow.*
He claps his hands.
In the village square,
we sit under plane trees.
We point at house-martins,
penny-wagtails, talk to a cat.
High on the church roof
men push wheelbarrows,
hurl slates down to a skip.
Inside the church it's dark.
The baby whispers,
puts his fingers to his lips.
I say your name, once.
You could start here.

If you could come back
you could have marmite on toast
we could lie down with the crumbs
you could splodge the newspaper with jam
you could sleep in late
get up and not have a plan
you could loll about in the bath
with the crossword
flip water all over the floor
stretch out on the sofa
eat chocolate ice-cream
you could kick your boots off
just inside the door
you could wear old shorts
grow week-end whiskers
flick banana chips at the dogs
you could watch rugby all day
spill your beer when they score
drink two bottles of red wine
you could come to bed late
bang about in the room
you could fall across the bed
and snore you could snore
if you could come back

amazon.co.uk

At amazon.co.uk you still live.
When I log on, they say, hello A.G. Sizer,
welcome back; as if it were that simple.
They say, if you are not A.G. Sizer,

click here. I never do. I read,
We have recommendations for you
or*, thank you for shopping with us,*
here are suggestions for your next visit.

Increasingly, you are reading poetry,
writers you didn't previously like.
I want to ask you what you thought of
Housekeeping. Did you weep when she

talks about longing and wild strawberries?
Do you remember the taste, blood red,
but rough on your tongue? Where you are,
with your books, are there strawberries?

Customers who bought, Housekeeping
also bought, Death of the Heart,
was one of them you? They also bought
Long Life. You would have done too.

Carpet

Today, I'm clear, I'm focused,
I'm driving up the hill between the traffic cones,
I'm going to buy a carpet.
I know the size and I'm thinking about the colour.
I think a new carpet will make a difference,
when you appear, in the carpet,
and I don't know how to do my life anymore
and I can't see the car in front and why
do you do this to me, all the time,
why can't you wait until the evening
when I'm on my own and why can't you
just let me buy a carpet, because now
I don't care about the carpet, I don't care
if I never see a carpet again. It's Friday,
so maybe I'll buy an Independent,
with the book bit, but I've probably
read them all anyway and I don't
want to know what's on T.V.
and then I think, if it's Friday,
then it's the week-end and it's another
week-end without you and I don't know
what to do with week-ends anymore
and I'm tired. I'm tired of week-ends,
I'm tired of newspapers, televisions,
and I'm tired of carpets, but I buy one
anyway and tie it to the roof of the car
and drive home slowly, because,
at the end of today, I'll know I've done
something. I've bought a carpet.

You don't know what you've got til it's gone

I'm in the shed, sorting nails by length
and size of head, brass handles into bags,
rawlplugs into browns and greys,
ten shades of wood stain, white spirit,
brushes, flat pencils, fillers, glue.
You have hoarded sash cords,
pulleys, bike parts, fish hooks, hinges,
the internal organs of a clock.
Your radio is inches thick with sawdust,
inside one of the compartments,
Del Shannon waits to sing.
Our bikes have four flat tyres,
my pedal's stuck between your spokes.
I slide my hand inside your cherry coloured
coat and find a pocket full of shot;
you who never shot anything, except
once, famously, took a catapult to a squirrel
then rushed outside because you'd hit it
in the leg. I find a piece of perished sling.
I lift down a caddy full of golf clubs,
and your rackets. I unzip the powdery cover
of "The Prince" and find two new balls
tucked against the strings. I think
I must have given away your squash bag
with your shoes, but don't know when.
I blow the shavings off your router, open
the little wooden set with all its heads.
We bought this from a widow,
whose husband didn't live to use it.
I think about her packing it back
with its unread instructions, its picture
on the cover of the box. She also
packed back a circular saw, but you
already had one and hers was dear.
I wade through the drill bits, stumble
on the mitre saw that nearly betrayed us

when we ran away to Dublin and left it
in my boot. It's quiet. I've been playing
Joni Mitchell. She's been asking Paradise
to put up a parking lot, but she's stopped
and I'm done. I shut the door, wonder if
I'll ever need a lost head nail. No-one knows.

Portwrinkle

We drive the coast road home,
drenched, and thick with salt.
The car stinks of dog and oarweed.
A swift mist bowls across the fields,
swamping sheep and farmsteads,
pulling in the day to sudden evening.
My indicator flashes to tell me
I've got no petrol in the tank.
I've got no money in the Bank
and no lover, but half an hour ago
the October sun blazed across the sea
as we leapt through pools of toothed wrack
kelp fronds and limpet. We found dulse,
hairweed, thongweed, Gulls' feathers,
a mermaid's purse, the empty egg case
of a whelk. I caught a shanny in my hands.
The tide snatched at the sand
so it appeared we drifted back and forth,
although we knew we stood quite still.
We danced in mock terror of the waves,
the roar and roll, and fell upon each other,
laughing. We let ourselves get wet, then wetter.
We squeezed the day like an orange
or a wet sock, hoping you could see.

Taking the long way
For Lynne

The long road home is pale rose, moonlit.
Dartmoor holds its hills and frosted thistles
dark against the sky. I drive too fast, wanting,
perhaps, to take off, to lift up into the hazy,
pleated distance, to go nowhere, to find
myself in uncharted water, not lost, but finding
a different way, a way without a North and South,
without the pull of evening, the way a plane climbs
until you sit above the clouds and surrender,
nothing you can do but be there,
stretched with fatigue and thinking
there are women who sail single-handed
around the world, who climb, who dive,
but nothing is more terrifying than standing still
with both feet solid on the ground.

In the time of rain

I dream of high winds, tall trees, then realise
that the sound outside is rushing water.
The river, swollen, trebling its size,
finding its old way, galloping, gathers
the fields in, rips at dead branches, snatches
the moorhens' half-made nest, spoils the fishing
grounds of the heron, the egrets I watch
at breakfast, their heads cocked as they listen
to the shallows. Days of rain are forecast.
I wade through them, think of building a boat
to save myself. I had hoped, at the last,
for a different river. I had hoped
the two of us, quarantined together,
would sail under the flag of cholera.

February
for Alyss

It's dark. You stand outside my door
with a camellia. I am horrified, not because
you're there, but because I have forgotten.
I have forgotten that it's February.
I haven't turned that page.
I haven't moved into this year yet.
I am at home, but in my dog clothes
and my socks. There's nothing
in the fridge or in the cupboards.
Both dogs are noisy, and in season,
so there's a mop and metal bucket.
You have elegant deserts from Waitrose.
I have no beer.
I can't believe that it's February.
February wants love, wants to hear
birdsong, wants to stretch its days out
into evening, wants to forget the drip
drip of its melancholy trees,
wants its ponds to boil with frog-spawn,
its herons to dance across the fields in pairs.
February paints its shop-fronts crimson,
promises forever, wants us to take
our clothes off, out of doors.
I bring in logs and light a fire.
We talk of loss and how the future
has shrunk to mean tomorrow;
yet, we talk of silver birch and cherries,
planting our sweet peas in guttering,
and the vegetables we'll grow this year.

March

Two black flutes tell me geese squat
in the marshy clumps of marigold.
I hold my breath, watch the dogs run past,
snuffling, hell-bent on early evening rabbit.
An empty train clatters by, but can't distract them.
In Roseanne's wood there's cherry blossom,
a sudden gift on yesterday's bare trees.
There are wind-flowers, now, among the aconite.
Buzzards cruise the sky, calling through the canopy
on the top hill where the coroner's clerk found a signal
to tell me what happens next. What happens next
is March, the third March, ready or not.
I climb the gate, the dogs slip through the hedge
and as I trudge the river bank, they swim upstream,
heads and tails above the string weed,
which soon will break white stars across the water.
Soon the garlic will come, stitchwort, campion,
and Graham will let his cows out.
We'll have to walk the road because the dogs
can't be trusted and I'm nervous of the bull.
It's seventeen degrees. I'm in my shirt-sleeves.
Last week it snowed. What happens next,
nobody knows, except the dogs, who wait
patiently, lined up beside the hose.

April

The dry cows are in the bottom field,
pressing at the gate. They watch
their abundant sisters pick their way, sway
across the hill's ridge. Their calls have all
the loneliness of evening, the loss of light.
Abandoned, they turn towards the trees.
I lean on the end fence, watch the night
come down, the first stars, the milky moon.
Behind me, the pinks and purples
of the garden hush, the tree of paradise
lowers its split trunk to the camellias,
blossom drifts in forgotten heaps
along the ground. April has given too much,
too soon. There was something parched
and frantic in the sun. Now the hawthorn
struggles with its weight of lace,
multitudes of bluebells drift in dappled light.
By the top hedge there's half a song-thrush egg,
black speckles on a stunning blue.
The new white hens with speckled necks
are in the campion, making their way
through the apple trees. I want to tell you
all this. I want to walk through my back door
into the light of a warm room and tell you

How to Save a Life

High tide. I pay the ferryman,
cross the water to where we were.
I take the church road,
its ox-eye daisies, its convolvulus,
its pink and white parsley.
The high hedges hide all promise
of the sea. I see us in a chill
May sun. This is another June.
I pull away from the visitors,
their thick socks, their boots,
their waterproof maps.
I drive to run out of road,
the unmapped miles of dog-rose,
honeysuckle and golden vetch
stretching for the sun. It rains.
I pull over in a muddy gateway
for a tractor. We exchange
the briefest nod, the slight
hand signal that says, we live here
and we travel with a purpose.

I turn for home,
rock the car with The Fray,
And I would have stayed up with you all night,
had I'd known how to save a life.

oh my love   the lilies are closing for the night
the sun has climbed into the tall trees

deep shadows hide the borders
shrug themselves across stone steps

only the wild rose shines pink and blows about
as the air changes from afternoon to evening

a cat stalks the perimeter of the house
hangs around the open door but will not enter

a cow calls another answers small birds settle
into hedges a train rides on the viaduct

it is June the day is leaving   all this happens
regardless of who lives who dies who watches

Wild Works
Dolcoath Mine. July

You arrive at dusk. There is music,
saffron cake, laughter. You watch
the stars come up across the moor.
The air is heavy with buddlia.
There is a first nip of autumn.
You travel with Orpheus
to the ends of the earth,
across the river, down to Hades.
Blue fire blazes at your feet,
then everywhere. You are asked
to record what your hands
most want to remember or, perhaps,
what your eyes most want to forget.
You leave this at the gate.
You have to let go of everything,
your clothes, even your language,
cut out your heart -
until Persephone comes,
in her emerald dress, singing,
and pleads for you. From time to time
lit trains of ordinary people pass through
on the far horizon. They have no idea
what's going on. You watch Orpheus
bargain for Eurydice, and carry her,
high on his shoulders, going home.
You watch him lose her.
It is dark, just the moon and the music.
He will set off again, and so will you.

August

It's 2 am.

I watch her launch herself to her feet,
a wisp of gold and bone.

The night is laden with lilies, lemon balm.
The moon is in Pleiades.

I lean against the wall between the peach
and the espaliered pear tree.

She is snuffing out, slowly.
Call her.

The night is full of small noise.
There are stars falling through Perseus.

I count them, arbitrarily, since I don't know
when they started, and I'm too tired

to stand here, barefoot, till the end.

September

For weeks the weather's held - dog days -
the woods stuffed with fruit, haws the size of sloes,
berries on the wayfaring trees, the colour

of Christmas. I feast amongst the brambles,
my mouth black, my fingers purple.
I linger by the river to watch for geese

or the single heron that lifts and takes itself up.
One night I sliced my hand with a sharp knife
I didn't see coming, and was appalled to think

I never considered myself to be in any danger -
though I often stumble into furniture
at night, when I forget I've moved it.

I dream of moving. Last night I packed
all my books, ran downstairs to say goodbye.
You were to follow. You stooped to kiss me.

Under the palms of my hands, I felt the dark
patches of sweat between your shoulder blades
and in the small of your back. When I said,

I love you, I spoke it into your mouth,
and woke, startled. You stayed with me
until I boiled water for tea and knew

you'd never come. Every morning,
for more than two years, I wrote to you
on waking, notebook after notebook.

Now, it's easier to write about September.
Some days, just to think about writing is to
open the palm of my hand with that knife.

October

The moon is furred with cold as I drive
three hundred miles southwest,
M6, M5, A38,   then cross the water.
The moon moves from right to left,
right again, hangs in half and orange.

I tag tail-light after tail-light. Bob Harris
plays Country, The Be Good Tanyas,
Alison Krauss sings with Robert Plant.

When I get home, I could watch
your last movements on a tape,
or you at 21, in a maroon velvet suit,
hamming up the Walker Brothers.
I could read every letter you wrote.
I could lie in the dark, try to
conjure up your face or fit myself
to the hot curve of your back.

There will be a frost on the grass in the morning.
I will be glad I brought the hollyhocks in.
It will be time to plant tulips and, in the gospel
according to my first father-in-law,
I could enjoy parsnips now.

Cartography
November

Some days I need to get lost,
to leave the path and climb
through trees to find the sun.

For a while I'll try to locate us,
search out highest points, take
bearings from the contours

of the hills. The pines new
perspective change my boundaries,
and I stumble on a barn

I've never seen before,
so I surrender to not knowing,
let the light lead me to the wild

edge of fields, set aside
and drenched in green,
Paradise to a rolling dog

who has her own geography.
She lifts her nose to map
vixen, rabbit, deer. Her ears

chart jays, a solitary buzzard,
hen pheasant in the stubble.
Out of sight, she sees me always

can return in a minute,
should she care to, and while
I watch my footing in the leaf mulch

she waits where the wind rips through
the chestnuts, where the days hurry
to get shorter, where I find I've arrived

at the far side of the apple orchard
and understand how to get us home.

December Song

This is the year's last gasp,
winter's whisper in the grass,
the fierce yellow of the gorse.

The sea pulls out to meet the sky
and soon, all there is of you
will be painted with that blue

of distance; the distant sheep,
fields of crows, the empty train,
and all that will remain

will be a locket on a chain
a photograph by a bed
the long night ahead

the sun sliding behind the hill,
the river, spun glass and still,
the white waiting moon

the last light wanting to be gone.

At the Gate

I won't know how or when, but I'll know
for certain that you'll see my face,
the blurred outline in the Dash 8
window, marvelling at the Pyrenees or the snow-
fall across the Alps, or perhaps I'll be in bed
becoming more and more ill,
then, when my body's completely still,
you'll start running or flying ahead
of me, whatever it is you need to do
to be there at the gate,
even if I'm late, you'll wait,
and because of you, I'll have no
baggage to reclaim, nothing to declare
and you'll be there, you'll be there.